CW00921202

I READ! YOU READ!

Child's Turn to Read

Adult's Turn to Read

WE READ ABOUT

Citizenship

Tracy Vonder Brink and Madison Parker

Table of Contents

CITIZENSHIP 3

WORDS TO KNOW 22

INDEX 23

COMPREHENSION QUESTIONS 23

SEAHORSE PUBLISHING

Parent and Caregiver Guide

Reading aloud with your child has many benefits. It expands vocabulary, sparks discussion, and promotes an emotional bond. Research shows that children who have books read aloud to them have improved language skills, leading to greater school success.

I Read! You Read! books offer a fun and easy way to read with your child. Follow these guidelines.

Before Reading

- Look at the front and back covers. Discuss personal experiences that relate to the topic.
- Read the *Words to Know* at the back of the book. Talk about what the words mean.
- If the book will be challenging or unfamiliar to your child, read it aloud by yourself the first time. Then, invite your child to participate in a second reading.

During Reading

CHILD Have your child read the words beside this symbol. This text has been carefully matched to the reading and grade levels shown on the cover.

ADULT You read the words beside this symbol.

- Stop often to discuss what you are reading and to make sure your child understands.
- If your child struggles with decoding a word, help them sound it out. If it is still a challenge, say the word for your child and have them repeat it after you.
- To find the meaning of a word, look for clues in the surrounding words and pictures.

After Reading

- Praise your child's efforts. Notice how they have grown as a reader.
- Use the *Comprehension Questions* at the back of the book.
- Discuss what your child learned and what they liked or didn't like about the book.

Most importantly, let your child know that reading is fun and worthwhile. Keep reading together as your child's skills and confidence grow.

Citizenship

CHILD

A citizen is a member of a country.

U.S. citizens are also known as Americans.

Citizens make up a country's population.
ADULT

All people born in the United States are its citizens.

Children of Americans are also U.S. citizens.

This is true even if they are born in another country.

CHILD

U.S. citizenship through acquisition happens when a person is born in another country to parents who are Americans.

ADULT

Immigrants are people from other countries who move to the U.S.

They may choose to become U.S. citizens.

They must follow steps to do so.

CHILD

Before they can begin the process of becoming a citizen, an **immigrant** must be a permanent resident of the U.S. for at least five years.

ADULT

They learn about the United States.

They must pass a test.

They promise to be good citizens.

Then, they become Americans.

U.S. citizenship through naturalization happens when an immigrant takes the steps to become a citizen. This takes about 18 to 24 months.

Americans have **rights**.

CHILD

They can **vote**.

People who are not citizens cannot vote.

The 19th Amendment was added to the U.S. Constitution in 1920. It said that all U.S. citizens have the **right** to **vote**.

ADULT

Americans vote for the president and other leaders.

Some jobs require workers to be citizens.

Only Americans may be elected as leaders.

CHILD

In order to serve in Congress as a U.S. Senator, a person must have been a U.S. citizen for at least nine years.

ADULT

Only people born in the United States may become president.

Citizens have the right to free speech.

And they can **worship** the way they want.

CHILD

The Bill of Rights was added to the U.S. Constitution in 1791. It gave citizens the right to speak freely and **worship** freely. It also guaranteed the right to a fair trial if a citizen is accused of a crime.

ADULT

Citizens also have **responsibilities**.
CHILD

They choose leaders.

They pay **taxes**.

Taxes fund the U.S. government. A percentage of each citizen's salary goes to the government.
ADULT

The government uses tax money to pay for things.

040

Department of the Treasury—Internal Revenue Service

U.S. Individual Income Tax Re

year Jan. 1–Dec. 31, 2013, or other tax year beginning

Last name

irst name and initial

Last name

oint return, spouse's first name and initial

ne address (number and street). If you have a P.O. box, see in

ty, town or post office, state, and ZIP code. If you have a foreign addr

Foreign country name

Filing Status

ck only one

1	☐	Single
2	☐	Married filing jointly (ev
3	☐	Married filing separate
		and full name here. ▶

Citizens obey laws.

They take care of each other.

They help take care of their community.

Citizens might help their communities by cooking and serving meals for people in need. They might pick up trash at rivers and parks.

They also work to make their community a better place to live.

A country needs good citizens.

CHILD

Responsible citizens take pride in their country. They help make everyone who lives in the country feel safe and happy.

ADULT

Words to Know

immigrants (IH-muh-grunts): people who come to a different country to make a new home

responsibilities (ruh-spawn-suh-BI-luh-tees): things people are expected to do

rights (rites): things a person is allowed to do under the law

taxes (TAK-suz): money that people pay to the government

vote (voht): to make a choice for or against someone or something

worship (WUR-shup): to take part in a religious service

Index

Americans 3, 4, 8, 10, 12

citizen(s) 3, 4, 6, 8, 10, 12, 14,
    16, 18, 20, 21

community 18, 20

immigrant(s) 6, 8

leaders 10, 12, 16

right(s) 10, 14

Comprehension Questions

1. What are some rights American citizens have?
   a. the right to vote
   b. the right to worship the way they want
   c. both A and B

2. Who can become a leader in America?
   a. immigrants
   b. military members only
   c. American citizens

3. What is a citizen?
   a. a member of a country
   b. a member of a team
   c. a member of a club

4. True or False: People who are not citizens can vote.

5. True or False: Citizens must pay taxes.

Written by: Tracy Vonder Brink and Madison Parker
Design by: Kathy Walsh
Editor: Kim Thompson

Library of Congress PCN Data
We Read About Citizenship / Tracy Vonder Brink and Madison Parker
I Read! You Read!
ISBN 979-8-8873-5198-8 (hard cover)
ISBN 979-8-8873-5218-3 (paperback)
ISBN 979-8-8873-5238-1 (EPUB)
ISBN 979-8-8873-5258-9 (eBook)
Library of Congress Control Number: 2022945525

Printed in the United States of America.

Photographs/Shutterstock: Cover ©topseller: Cover,
Pg 1 ©Tuari Media, ©Lightspring, ©Vertes Edmond
Mihai: Pg 4-21 ©Lightspring: Pg 3 ©Monkey Business
Images: Pg 5 ©Zurijeta: Pg 7 ©Diego G Diaz: Pg 9
©Kim Kelley-Wagner: Pg 11 ©vesperstock: Pg 13
©Sean Locke Photography: Pg 15 ©Chanyanuch
Wannasinlapin: Pg 17 ©Eastside Cindy: Pg 19
©Dmytro Zinkevych: Pg 20 ©Rawpixel.com

Seahorse Publishing Company

www.seahorsepub.com

Published in the United States
Seahorse Publishing
PO Box 771325
Coral Springs, FL 33077